MS, God and Me explores my personal struggle living with Multiple Sclerosis, including bouts of mental illness, alongside my own relationship with Jesus Christ, the Son of God, throughout this time. I would like to try and give hope to others struggling with chronic disease, or facing the difficult issues that life has dealt them.

'Steve tells his story of MS with both honesty and hope. Not pulling any punches, he speaks candidly of his struggles with depression, anxiety, psychosis, pain, despair and separation from God. There are no promises of healing or resolution within these pages; instead, Steve shows us how to cling to God in the midst of devastating circumstances, and how God sometimes answers. Those living with chronic illness can take great encouragement from Steve's testimony. This is a powerful story of the myriad of ways God's grace can shine in our darkness like stars in the night sky.'

Steph Penny, psychologist and author of Surviving Childlessness

MS, God and Me
A Christian's Journey

Stephen Hatton

Journey Publishers

MS, God and Me: A Christian's Journey

ISBN 978-1-7636022-0-5

Email:
Stephen.n.hatton@gmail.com

Many thanks to my dad Neville Hatton for editing this book, and to my wife Richelle Hatton for inspiration, flow, and format of the book. I am deeply grateful to you both.

Contents

Introduction

Hi, my Name is Stephen Hatton. I am 61 years old. My wife is Richelle. I thank God for her. We have been married for 31 years. My wife and I do not have children.

This book will take you through some of the struggles and joys that we have faced over a 26 years period, coping with **Multiple Sclerosis**, an acquired disease which affects the nervous system, in particular the brain and spine. Throughout, I have inter-woven poems and songs that have helped me express the grief I've felt over the years.

God is the Creator, my God and my Lord, my comfort, my peace, and my praise. This book and the poems it contains are a reflection of life's struggle and how God has led me through each day. After the initial shock, then denial and the 'never-accept' syndrome, I have come to the realization that I must learn to live with and manage this unpredictable disease.

Myelin is the protective sheath that covers the nerves. In people suffering from Multiple Sclerosis (MS), this sheath depletes, meaning messages from the brain don't always go where they're supposed to go. In particular, MS affects the nerves in the brain and the spinal cord.

I was lying down when I had a sudden urgency to pray. God's voice said, "I am going to take you through a time of darkness when you will not see me or know me". Before me I saw a gentle slope. Suddenly, it dropped into utter darkness. My heart sank. Then came these words, "I will bring you into a green pasture". A line went almost vertically straight up. I saw a beautiful green field that seemed to go on forever, brightly lit by the sun. What did this mean?

Chapter 1:

Early Years

I was born in the town of Madang, Papua New Guinea, then a Territory of Australia, in 1962. I am an Australian citizen. My sister Christine was born 19 months before me, and my brother Barry 19 months after me. My second sister Michelle was born 7 years later in Australia. During this time in PNG, my dad was a teacher, becoming Headmaster of Tusbab High School in Madang. In 1969, he was appointed as Principal of the first Senior High School for New Guineans at Form 5 level. This was located at Sogeri, 50 km from Port Moresby, near the start of the Kokoda Trail. I don't remember much about New Guinea days. (Note that one of the symptoms of MS is memory loss in some people).

My parents had purchased a 3 bedroom Unit in East Lakes which we moved into following our return to Australia in 1970. Dad became a Lecturer in Education at Sydney University. Mum was bringing up us kids, and teaching in a nearby Catholic Primary School. She had trained as a teacher at Balmain. I went to the primary school at Daceyville where a few significant things happened to me. I joined the Daceyville Primary School Brass Band directed by Mr. Fred Royal. We played at lots of venues and won competitions. I played a 'Bb Bass' Tuba, which I did enjoy.

We moved to Grays Point in Sutherland Shire in 1972. The suburb is about 50 minutes drive South of Sydney. Our home was located right on the edge of the Royal National Park. It is beautiful area, covered with bush, red and yellow Bottle Brush bushes, wattles, flowers and gum trees. Lower down in Grays Point is the Port Hacking River. Dad bought the house for $25,000. This was a lot for him. At that time you could only borrow 75% of the full payment. We lived opposite the Soccer Oval. There was a hill up to it, blocking our view. Beside the oval, on the right and behind it, was the Park itself, a perfect place for riding our push-bikes, walking and exploring. My brother loved the wildlife. He often caught poisonous snakes (Red-belly Blacks), as well as lizards called Water Dragons. On the south side of the Oval was Grays Point Primary School.

Mum's mother, Grandma Hadley, was a full-on Christian. She worked for the Christian Endeavour movement. She would also spend whole nights praying for us kids. One night when I woke up, she was not praying in English, but some other language. I have since learned that this is called praying in tongues. I believe Grandma's (and my parents') prayers for me helped shape the kind of Christian life I went on to experience.

Mum worked at East Hills (about 40 minutes drive from our place) as an English language teacher with Vietnamese immigrants. She always made time to welcome people as if they were her own best friends. I struggled a lot with this for a long time. She loved them just as she loved me. We did not have much, but my parents still gave away a lot to help people in need.

When we moved to Grays Point, I started school there in 4th class. I made good friends and loved my teacher, Mrs Hosie. She was very easy to talk with. I fell in love in about 6th class with Kerry. I put aftershave on a letter and gave it to her in an envelope. What I didn't know is that she had a boyfriend already. This persisted through to high school, and he became her husband. (I did get a letter from her later, explaining that she already had a boyfriend.)

I was just a normal kid who loved the outdoors and the bush. I joined the local Cub group and later the Scouts, at that time for boys only. I loved all the things we learned, like how to tie knots, how to camp and going out in boats. A friend of the scouts, Mr Brack, was a very gracious man. His wife Mary started the first Sunday School in Grays Point, which later became part of the Baptist Church established there. At his place we had a bottle drive to recycle old bottles. We used to pick up and sort heaps and heaps of bottles by hand. I do remember we had no gloves on while sorting the broken ones!

I rode my bike everywhere in the National Park. I must have been quite fit because I would ride for 1 to 2 hours each afternoon after school. I loved doing wheelies (lifting the front wheel off the ground, while balancing and riding along for 20 metres), plus jumps on my front sprung Nock and Kirby Special Bicycle. It was very heavy, about 8 kilograms, not like today's light weight bikes. One day I got enthusiastic and jumped off a high jump, about 1.5 metres high. When I landed the frame broke. I fell heavily to the ground, and was bleeding from my knees and ankles. I was more interested in riding than school and homework. This would continue all the way through Primary then into High School. We still had homework, though.

I have mixed memories of High School at Kirrawee. I started to put on some weight at High School and I hated Gymnastics because of this. With other students from my year, I was forced to jump on the benches and trampoline, although I made it very clear that I did not want to. On my very first attempt, I jumped from a mini trampoline up onto a bench, and instantly broke my finger! This reinforced my fear of Gymnastics and did not help improve my dislike of school.

On another occasion, I was riding my mountain bike down Wanganui Street, on the way home. It was a very steep hill, and as I tried to push on my back-pedal brakes, they just didn't work. Instead, I was thrown over the handlebars, landing on my backside. As I rode down the rest of the hill, I had an insane pain in my left finger. I looked and it was just dangling there. I went to the Doctor, just around the corner, and he reset it because it was broken.

At Kirrawee High, I did enjoy Technics 1 and 2 - Metal Work. I struggled with my other school subjects. Learning was hard work for me. I had trouble thinking and processing information. I left in year 10 at 16 years of age to go and find a job.

In 1979, our whole family of six went overseas for 12 months for Dad's first Sabbatical Leave. Initially, we went to America for 3 months, while he visited various universities there. Dad bought a motor home, and we drove over 3000 miles across the different states. We saw the Space Shuttle being moved from one town to another on the main road. It was on a special trailer with a driver at the back and the rear of the truck.

On this journey, I had a significant medical incident. There was a solar eclipse and the whole family watched it together. We all were careful not to look at it directly. Immediately afterwards, I completely lost sight in my left eye. I was scared and didn't understand what was going on. We went and saw a doctor and he thought I must have looked at the solar eclipse, causing the blindness, however, I had not. I knew better than that. Two weeks later, my sight partially returned as mysteriously as it had disappeared.

Later, we had 6 months in England. Christine and her friend Anne and I went to Austria for a trip as well. In England I did casual work as a builder's labourer. In the first few weeks, the ligaments between my fingers stretched from using a heavy wheelbarrow loaded with wet concrete. I joined a local gym in Nottingham to get fit. I was very strong as a result of all this work and working out!

I came back to Australia three months earlier than my parents, with Christine. I was interested in doing a trade, so I applied to Qantas to become an apprentice Ground Engineer, learning to maintain Jet aircraft. They were going to choose 2 people out of the thousand who applied and unfortunately they didn't choose me. My Uncle Frank, who worked for Utilux, an electronic manufacturing company, helped me choose an apprenticeship area – metal work because I had loved studying this at school. Then Uncle Ray and Peter Sigal, my next door neighbour, came to my aid, resulting in an apprenticeship as a Fitter and Machinist with General Motors Holden (GMH) at Pagewood in 1980. I really enjoyed working on the car assembly line. I learnt to machine metal, as well as weld and fabricate steel. GMH then closed down their operations at the end of that year. Mum found me an apprenticeship at Johnson Screens in nearby Kirrawee. I stayed there till the completion of my four-year term.

Around this time, I went to a Grays Point Baptist Church camp for youth at Fitzroy Falls Conference Centre. I really listened to the message about turning from living life my own way without God to become a new creation in Jesus Christ – A fresh spiritual start. A man at the camp was swearing a lot and raging around with a loud voice. One of the young people walked up to him and said, "In the Name of Jesus Christ, be silent". The noisy man fell to the ground and became quiet. I got scared that God was that powerful. That night I repented of my sin. I cried and confessed to God that I'd been trying to live life by myself. I became a believing Christian at the age of sixteen and a half.

When I turned 17, I wanted to build a fast VW off-road buggy. I had to buy one first. As I considered this, I visited the Christian Growth Centre at Sutherland. Well, actually it was then at Miranda, while they were erecting a new building. I visited this church and sat up the back for a few visits. One time, I was I quietly in my mind surrendering to God the desire to build a performance car. Suddenly, I stood to my feet and shouted out, "Lord, you've broken through by the power of your Spirit. My spirit is filled!" Some elders came around me to pray. I fell back, overwhelmed with God's love and the power of the Holy Spirit. I also started to pray in another language at this time. When I stood up I was filled with faith. A friend of mine, Mr Jones asked, "How do you feel?" My reply was, "I said I can drive the car home without keys!" This is what many Christians call baptism in the Holy Spirit. After this experience of the power of God's Spirit, I started to devour the Bible, the Holy Scriptures.

In 1984, I went to Sydney Missionary and Bible (nick-named 'Bridal') College at Croydon. I did a two-year diploma in Divinity and Mission. This involved cross cultural studies, youth work training and bible theology, with a small introduction to the original Greek language that the New Testament is written in. I do remember vividly the following incident from 1985. Bevan, the foreman from Johnson Screens, called me. He used to come up to me while I was working and swear using Christ Name to hurt me. It sure worked, for I felt a sword going through my heart every time! However, three years later he rang to tell me that his daughter had invited him to church. Bevan felt dirty and convicted by God during the service. So he came forward to put his trust in Jesus, and was filled with the Holy Spirit. He went on to tell me that as the foreman in another location, the men now called him "Jesus"!

I was interested in going overseas to be a missionary. However, it didn't eventuate, because I became unwell for a while. In 1986, I went to hospital for a minor operation on my right arm. It was there that I met Andrew K. He is Malaysian and has become a lifelong friend. I was privileged to be best man at his wedding to Christine. In 1987, I was accepted as Youth Worker at Gymea Anglican Church. This involved caring for the teenagers at church, as well as running a weekly youth group. A few weeks in, my Minister, Rev. Jack Derrett, asked me to teach Scripture in the local schools. This is where I learned to communicate effectively with children and youth. I taught at Gymea

Bay Primary from Year 1 (6 year olds) all the way to Year 6 (12 year olds), some classes at Kirrawee Primary, and year 7 (13 year olds) through to Year 10 (16 year olds) at both Gymea Technology High and Kirrawee High Schools. At the end of the year, as my contract was ending, I was encouraged by Jack to pursue teaching as a career.

It was in 1987 that I met Richelle. She attended the church where I was the youth worker and she was a member of the youth group. We did not go out or anything at this point, but we did enjoy talking to one another about all sorts of things.

Also, from time to time, I experienced unusual medical episodes. One time I couldn't get out of bed because my body was paralysed. This resolved the next day. Another time I experienced unexplained weakness in one leg. The doctor could not explain these symptoms and they all resolved relatively quickly. I soon forgot about them.

Chapter 2:

New Beginnings

In 1986-1990, I was too late applying to get into the Industrial Arts course at Sydney University, so I applied to the Catholic Teachers College at Castle Hill, where I trained to become a teacher. I chose to do Industrial Arts with a focus on Pastoral Care of students. This College offered a Diploma in Living Skills – Teaching, which included, Industrial Arts, Design and Technology and Religious Education. My health was relatively good back in 1988. But I still found theoretical concepts difficult to master. Rod, who was a good friend, helped me immensely. I am ever grateful to him.

In 1989, while I was at Teachers College, I was living at Pendle Hill, west of Sydney, and I was helping with the Youth Group at Pendle Hill Baptist Church. I went with the youth group to Katoomba Easter Convention, where I saw Richelle. Richelle was there with the youth group from Gymea Anglican Church. I went back with her to the place they were staying and caught up with many friends. Then Richelle came with me to where I was staying. When she walked in the door, one of the young girls called out, "That's your future wife!" Both of us were embarrassed and didn't know quite where to look. This was out of character for the young girl because she was usually very quiet.

We started dating after that and on our first date, Richelle drove all the way to Pendle Hill (about an hour's drive). She got a bit lost on the way. When she was stopped at some traffic lights, she rolled down her window and asked a motor bike rider beside her where the Great Western Highway was. He just pointed to a huge sign saying, "Great Western Highway". Somehow, she had ended up on the right road. She thanked him and rolled the window back up. I cooked dinner for Richelle at the house where I rented a room: chicken chasseur. She was very impressed. Then we went to watch the movie Beaches at Parramatta. We dated for about ten months, then got engaged. I wanted a 6 month engagement but Richelle was only 19 (I was 27) so her parents insisted we wait for 12 months before getting married.

1991 was a big year for us. I got my first teaching job at St Patricks College, a Catholic High School in Sutherland as an Industrial Arts and Design and Technology teacher, taking Years 7-10, that is, 13-17 year olds in co-ed classes. Richelle was in her final year of her Bachelor of Education training to become a primary school teacher. We both took a week off leading up to Easter so we could get married on 23 March. Each of us was quite well at the time, and really looking forward to our life together. At the reception, we were advised by my father to seek Jesus' Kingdom first in our marriage, and all the other things would be provided. God has indeed proved his faithfulness over and over again during 32 years of marriage.

Richelle turned 21 on our honeymoon, spent at Port Macquarie in New South Wales, so I went AWOL for several hours while I looked for a birthday cake to give her on the dinner cruise I had booked for that night. We did not have mobile phones back then and she didn't know where I was. All the cakes were sold out but I did eventually find one with little sugar mice on the top. It was very cute and delicious. I took it to the boat and they later surprised Richelle by bringing it out during dessert. She was amazed and finally understood what I had been up to all afternoon.

Teaching at High School level is a full-on job. I really enjoyed seeing students grow in their understanding of subject matter. We were also a pilot school for teaching the Design and Technology syllabus. We also needed to teach computing, using Apple Macintosh computers. Therefore, I enrolled in a 2-year Graduate Diploma in Computing from the University of New South Wales – Oatley Campus. Classes were conducted in the evening and covered both secondary students and adults.

I continued having some trouble with the vision in my left eye. It was as if a fine fish net were over it. I would see a word one moment, but it was gone in the next. A specialist in Ophthalmology in Sydney told me I was a hypochondriac and was making it all up about losing vision in my left eye. He looked into my left eye, but not further. Those close to me accepted his diagnosis at the time. I don't hold anything against them, though.

In 1993, I was referred to the Sydney Eye Hospital by Mr. C, my Optometrist in Gymea. Over a twelve-month period they tested my eyes. Each test came back negative but eventually led to a consultant Neurologist, who suspected that I had Multiple Sclerosis. Further tests were needed to confirm this tentative diagnosis.

At this time, Richelle and I considered buying land, with the requirement to build a house in 12 months. This was at Mount Annan, a 45-minute drive west from Sutherland. The land was $60,000 and a house a further $80,000. At the time, the going interest rate was 17%! In the end, we decided we just could not afford it. We could buy the land but not the house, as we only had my wage for a loan. At that stage, Richelle was a casual teacher trying to find permanent work. And banks did take into account the earnings of casual teachers. It would be another 14 years before we could get a home loan.

Being a teacher inevitably has times of extreme stress. Around 1993, I started to become very anxious while teaching. I was trying to keep up with learning and teaching new content, producing work for students, marking homework, maintaining the workshops at school and developing a possible year 11 and 12 Industrial Studies syllabus. As well, I was going to university, 30 minutes' drive from school and an hour from home at night, then driving the next day 25 kilometres to and from school. At the time, I was also jointly running a Bible study with my wife at Grays Point, although we lived at Bundeena, 30 kilometres away. And somewhere in all that I was seeking to be a good husband to my wife!

At the end of 1993, I ended up having a nervous breakdown. Everything was just too much. I was extremely anxious, shaking, and very distressed. My Consultant Neurologist sent me to the Prince of Wales Hospital for further tests. At the start they said I had anxiety plus, the direct result of my breakdown. I had a lot of pins with electrodes attached to them stuck in my head, numerous blood tests, and a lumbar puncture of my spine to extract some fluid. Then an MRI of the brain at Royal Prince Alfred Hospital confirmed my neurologist's initial diagnosis of Multiple Sclerosis (MS).

In January 1994, when the test results came back, the neurologist diagnosed me officially with Multiple Sclerosis. I was just 31 years old. The neurologist explained that the episode with my left eye when I was 16 was caused by optic neuritis, a deterioration of the optic nerve behind the eye, which the earlier specialist had not known to look for. Optic neuritis is a symptom of MS. The scans showed the optic nerve behind my left eye had depleted somewhat. It was so thin that my eyesight was permanently damaged. The MRI also showed that there were multiple scars on nerves in my brain, known as MS plaques. This diagnosis also explained all those weird symptoms I had experienced throughout my life. I felt relieved to finally have a diagnosis, but at the same time, I was distressed because of the new and changing symptoms I was experiencing. I also didn't really know what MS was and what it would mean for our future. The neurologist said there was nothing he could do and sent us home.

We contacted the MS Society, who sent a social worker, Lisa, who explained to us what MS actually is. MS is a disease of the central nervous system, affecting the brain and the spinal cord. Nerves are surrounded by a coating called myelin, rather like the way electrical wires are shielded by a plastic coating. In MS, the immune system attacks this coating and damages it, forming plaques or scars. These scars cause electrical signals from the brain to become confused, misdirected or lost. This process leads to the vast array of MS symptoms, which vary widely from person to person depending on where the nerves are damaged. At the time of my diagnosis, there were no treatments available at all. This was quite devastating, especially as my symptoms were becoming worse and quite severe.

I came apart. A nervous breakdown at the end of 1993, and a diagnosis of Multiple Sclerosis were just too much for me to cope with. I could not work. The school gave me 96 teaching days leave to try and recover. I didn't. I was shaking all over most of the time, very distressed and distraught. Not able to sleep, the severe fatigue was really getting me down. MS fatigue is not just feeling tired. It is having no energy to do anything and has a big impact on life. Being at home all the time was also a big challenge, but I just did not have the energy to go elsewhere. A hospital psychiatrist put me on a medicine called Tofranil to control anxiety. But it actually changed my behaviour and caused me to have suicidal tendencies. This medicine was increased every time I saw the psychiatrist at Prince of Wales Hospital.

I came off the medication at the suggestion of my mother, as she remembered that I had been given it as a baby and Tofranil had changed my behaviour then. I started to sleep again and felt much better in myself. With the help of an MS Society social worker, Lisa, who negotiated with the school, I was able to go back to part-time teaching. But it was very difficult for me and for the students. Later Sue, another person from the same Society, helped me accept that in order to survive, I had to care for myself first of all, and not be so focused others, as I had been for so many years.

At this time, a kind friend, David, emailed me the following 10 Christian reasons to live—My
wife; my church family at Gymea; people who still have not heard of Jesus Christ; so you can play your music for the Lord; because He who began a good work in you will be faithful to complete it; we are more than conquerors through Christ; Jesus is coming!; so that you can pray for me; I can pray for you; you can have kids then send them to my school to be taught music by me.

I also started to experience some serious side effects of the MS. The fatigue was so severe that I felt that my body was like a car battery, which would just keep on going flat. Sometimes I would not be able to get started in the morning, as I would wake exhausted – with the battery fully drained. I also had severe pain in my legs, body and head, which no medicine would touch. I had trouble with my water works. I would feel an urgent need to go to the toilet, no matter what I was doing. As a result, I was referred to Professor of Urology at Prince Henry Hospital.

This specialist told me that the S3 nerve in the lower spine was the cause of my agony. It would cause excruciating pain in my back-side and water works. Out of ten, it was an eleven. The Pain Team gave me eight tablets a day of Panedine Forte to try and lower the pain level. At that time, I was not eligible for Morphine as it was considered too addictive for me. They gave me two nerve blocks over a two-year period, to try and manage the excruciating pain in S3 nerve. The first one was effective, but the second one not as much. During one of these nerve blocks, I was unconscious, under a full general anaesthetic, when I involuntarily smashed the oxygen bottle with my right arm. I felt the needle go into the nerve. Later, after suffering a bad bruise along my arm, the surgeon told me that I was hypersensitive to pain as a result of Multiple Sclerosis. In 1995, Dr M diagnosed me with chronic MS, chronic pain, chronic anxiety, and clinical depression. I was on tricyclic medication at this time.

The doctor also told me one day, "You won't always be like this." I see this as a God incident. He had seen me very sick while treating me over a period of 6 years. Each day, I felt like I was dying inside. There seemed no hope. I feel God may have revealed this to him to give me hope at a very difficult time.

Many Christians were praying for me. A Catholic Christian from my school said to me, "I am storming heaven for you." People were trusting God for my full and complete healing. My church, Gymea Anglican, the Nuns at Calvary Hospital, where my mother worked as a social worker in Aged Palliative Care, the St Andrew's Cathedral Healing Ministry and Prayer Mountain, along with many others, were praying for me day and night. I couldn't pray for myself. I was too exhausted with the debilitating fatigue.

I can't believe I did this now, but in January, 1995, despite my illness, I applied to work with the Menai Board of Christian Education, which was placing a part-time Christian Studies Teacher in the State High School at Menai. They wanted a professionally trained teacher and Bible College graduate to fill the role. This was an invaluable experience. About seven churches in the area were represented on the Board. They prayed for me, and with the laying on of hands sent me to work in this school. The beauty of this experience was that these Christians supported and cared for me. They urged me to keep on, all while I was still quite unwell. The school's staff members were also very helpful, especially two senior teachers and the principal.

With God's help, I wrote the first syllabus for Christian Studies, and participated in the life of the school. The students were helpful and encouraging to me. The school's pastoral care support was very involved. In the first week of teaching, I informed the classes I had Multiple Sclerosis. One of the students asked, 'What do we do if you fall over?' Another student said, "Walk over him of course!" I laughed a lot. It was a great ice breaker. The students were good to me. Life went on at the school. I even did a few days of casual teaching per week.

As a representative of the Menai Board, I worked for only for two days each week. This was a moving time so far as helping students went. One girl in year 7 came to me and said, "Sir, I have Cystic Fibrosis. I've been told I will die within 12 months. Can you pray with me?" We both cried. Another girl in year 9 came and said, "Can you tell me why God is making me blind?" I did not have any answer as I was asking the same question. She had been walking across the playground and was hit by a stray basketball on the left side of her head. She instantly went blind in her left eye, and her right eye was deteriorating as well. This was a rewarding but a challenging time. I was glad to be able to share my faith but at the same time felt debilitated by MS.

Soon after this I became very ill. I collapsed a few times while teaching the students. My speech became rather slurred (that is, very slow, with words just blending together). The students were finding this time and my obvious suffering difficult. I was using two walking sticks to assist me with walking at this time. I prayed to God specifically about my health.

It was September 1995 when the unexpected answer came. A friend, David M, rang me from Port Macquarie and said, "Hey Steve, I was praying and felt God wanted you to know it's OK for you not to work". The amazing thing is that same week, another Christian from Menai Anglican, whom I did not know personally, rang and said he wanted me to know that it's OK not to work. I cried with gratitude. At my church on the following Sunday, Alex, a lovely Christian lady said to me directly, "It's OK for you not to work." On the spot I cried and cried at God's amazing answer to my prayer. With so many fears that were too big for me, God gave me a song and music to a sing out my thanks to Him. At the time, I was meditating on Psalm 142 in the *New International Bible* – A prayer for help – and wrote these words.

You are there Lord

1995©Stephen N. Hatton

You are there beside me, You are there, oh Lord.
You are there to catch me, even when I fall.

Even when I'm down, Lord, You meet me in my need.
You care and sustain me, and help me through my
grief, oh Lord.

CHORUS
Thank You Father for your precious love,
Thank You Jesus for the work you have done (on the
Cross),
Thank You Spirit for the freedom to serve.
Oh my God, thank You for your love.

Your love Lord is upon me. Your love sets me free.
Your blood was shed for me upon that rugged tree.
You're a pillar for the weak, O Lord. Your strength
helps me through.
The tears that I cried Lord, are precious, very precious
to You.

I put in my resignation to the Board, who accepted
it. They graciously gave me one month on full pay and
prayed for Richelle and me. God really encouraged me
through them. God closed one door of ministry and
opened another, setting me free to serve him despite
the MS. I also rested to try and recuperate.

This was a challenging time financially as Richelle
was still working as a casual teacher. The amazing
thing was that just as I had to give up work, Richelle
was offered a block of full-time casual work for 12
months on a maternity leave position. I believe this was
God's timing to provide for us. We also rented a unit
in Gymea and the rent was not put up for the whole

sixteen years we lived there, another blessing from God. While this was a tough time, we always had enough and were blessed by the generosity of our family and church family.

Members of my church at Gymea were invaluable at this time with their prayers and practical support. I wrote a letter to the church asking them if they could buy me an electric scooter. This would assist me to get around independently. Richard, one of the wardens and a businessman said, "It's not whether we can raise the money, it's what will we do with the excess?" They worked very hard, some people even giving up part of their wages, and did indeed raise more money than was needed. With these funds, they bought me an electric scooter with a canopy to give me freedom to get around, even in the sun or rain.

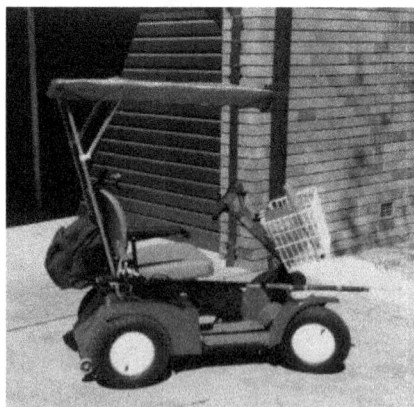

One day, I drove the scooter on the footpath, on a large loop, from north Gymea to Caringbah and back again, about 20 kilometres return, using almost all the charge. I even went fishing on the scooter 4 kilometres from home! It had a 40 kilometre range on one battery charge, at a speed of up to 10 kilometre an hour. A ladies bible study gave us groceries at this time too. Others gave money, or loaned holiday houses and their homes to help us have breaks, including one down the coast and another up at Leura in the Blue Mountains, 60 minutes drive west of Sydney. One person, Craig, lent us his Mazda sports car with a full tank of petrol, to drive to Palm Beach (about 60kms away) for a treat. It was a soft top, so the roof was taken off. It was sunny that day and we had a ball in his car. I am so grateful for all these acts of kindness. There are so many people whom I am grateful to for their constant prayers and support for over 25 years. God only knows who they are and where they live, in Sydney, across Australia, and all over the World.

Late in 1995, I could walk just 40 steps at the most aided by my two walking sticks before collapsing. At other times a wheelchair was necessary. There was so much weakness, fatigue, exhaustion and severe pain in my legs. Cognitively, I was having great difficulty processing information. My thoughts were a bit scrambled, as was my brain with any matter requiring any careful consideration. I had difficulty speaking and understanding people. At other times my speech was slurred, and I'd say words that didn't make sense. Other strange things started to happen. One day I was walking and started to go sideways, aided by my walking sticks, just like a crab. Richelle came to assist me with going the right way, straight ahead. I was very confused at the time. I was trying to get through each moment, then each day, one step at a time.

Early in 1996, two Christians at Cooma Music Convention prayed for me in a drama and prayer workshop. One lay down, while the other knelt down and said, "Rest in the Lord". Then later they spoke with me. At this time, I was unable to participate in activities and was terribly fatigued. I was lying down in my bedroom, wondering where this illness was headed. For two years it had just been getting worse and worse. The world was racing by me. I thought I was the only one suffering like this. I thought I had Progressive MS. I began to really hate MS. I felt that MS sucked! I really did not like it, the constant unpleasantness in my body and my brain. Some MS sufferers call MS their friend. Not me. One day I said to God, "You had the Lord Jesus live on earth for 33 years, then go into heaven. Here I am, suffering so horribly at 34 and there seems to be no end in sight."

Addiction Broken

Cathy B, a friend from church, kept urging me in my distressed state to go and see her boss, Canon Jim Holbeck of the Healing Ministry at St Andrew's Cathedral, Sydney. One day in 1997, Richelle and I agreed to go. We caught the train in. Jim was kind and full of compassion. As we talked, he discovered that I had an addiction to looking at not so helpful websites on the internet. This had been going on for 10 years. I had tried just about everything I could to break the urge to see more. I was in terrible bondage. I had sought help from Christian Ministers, as well as from God. But I had kept going back to the filth, while feeling terrible shame in my heart.

As Canon Jim prayed in the Spirit, we waited on God. The Lord revealed a curse that had been placed on me 10 years earlier. God reminded me of a time when I was a youth minister and was teaching Scripture in a local primary school in 1987. Over a few weeks, I had noticed that a year 4 student aged 10 was not in the class. I saw him in the playground one day and asked why he was not coming. He told me, "My mum is a spiritist and she prays against you." Canon H prayed in the name of Jesus Christ that the chains of the curse be broken from this child of God. He also anointed me with oil and prayed that God heal me of the MS. I did not think God would do that for me. Three days later I realized that I was completely free of this bondage. God had set me free, just as if I were a new Christian. At this time, God filled me afresh with His Holy Spirit. Such peace and joy!

Shortly after this, I was filled with God's Holy Spirit and I was renewed after being set free. My friend Ken invited me to his workplace in inner city Redfern. He warned me not to go near a certain man, who was always on about his drugs. He had been in prison many times. We were standing there talking when this man walked up to us. He showed us some of his marihuana. God urged me to pray and say with authority, "I bind you Satan in the name of Jesus Christ." Immediately the man broke down, in tears and said, "I see a cross with Jesus Christ hanging on it." He did not know what this meant. Therefore, we talked to him and explained that Jesus Christ came as a man but at the same time fully God. Jesus cared for the sick, the addicted, and the suffering. Finally, his enemies crucified him on a cross, which means he was killed and put up on a wooden cross for all to see. This was an act of love to deal with people's sins or rebellion against God and to set them free to love him. Jesus died, was buried, then he came back to life three days later. This is the Good News of Christianity.

This man responded to this message of love and forgiveness, as we explained the significance of his vision of Jesus Christ on the cross. Since he was still at work, I gave him a small Bible I had with me and advised him to start by reading the book of Mark. This describes the life of Jesus. God is so good at releasing people from their sin and bondage. I went home on the train rejoicing. Ken has encouraged me a lot over the years. He is indeed an invaluable friend.

Chapter 3:

MS Treatments and Symptoms

Up to this time, I had not been eligible for any of the MS treatments then available. The MS was active in my brain, and not in a limb, which meant I did not meet the criteria for accessing treatment. I was seeing a professor of neurology at Royal Prince Alfred MS Clinic. Soon afterwards, I was referred to see an MS specialist at Liverpool Hospital. She had empathy for me and gave me methyl-prednisone as a treatment. This involved going to Ambulatory Care at Liverpool Hospital for five days in a row. The medication was put into a drip and I had to sit there for several hours each day while it went into my system. This treatment aims to stop the swelling of nerves and therefore reduce the frequency of MS attacks. This treatment continued on and off for about two years. This treatment did not appear to do a great deal but it was better than doing nothing.

Each day I would experience up to ten different MS symptoms—blurred vision, exhausting fatigue, severe pain in my head, legs, or skin, bouts of weakness, mood swings, anxiety and

/or depression. I would start the day feeling reasonable, then within an hour I'd feel very distressed as I would suddenly become severely depressed. It was too much some days, but I persevered, taking it one hour at a time. I wrote the thoughts below, trying to work out why, early one morning.

WHAT'S THE POINT?

©Stephen N. Hatton 25/01/1997 at 5am

To Jesus,

Where is there meaning in this strife we call life?
I cannot fathom reason, purpose, or being,
when you cannot work for reasons beyond the seen,
or you feel like the sky is falling,
a feeling of absolute despair.

What is the point of it all? Who really knows?
You may offer your opinion, from a smug point of view.
That's fair enough.
But I am speechless, lacking direction.
There's got to be a use-fullness for me.

Life was once… but I can't think like that now.
Survival is one day, even an hour at a time.
But I can't help but think about what is ahead.
Appears three years brain dead.
Meaningless, meaningless, what's the point of it all?

Father God, I will rest in You.
I have nowhere else to go.
Show me how to serve when all I want to do is give up.
Help me to resist temptation, especially lust.
Lord Jesus, help me to trust, trust, trust.

Jesus Christ purchased me as His own.
My name was carved on that cross, written in His
blood.
Love cannot be defined, but in You.
Love You are, love unchanging, love divine.
Help me to know You and the abundant life You give.

from Stephen

Despite the many challenges, my faith in God helped me to cope and keep on going.

When I was diagnosed with MS there were not really any treatments available. Ongoing research led to more and more medications being trialled and made available. My neurologist was involved in this research and had early access to new treatments, which was a huge blessing for me. My neurologist put me on

Betaferon, a brand new medication, which required self-given injections twice a week. I was on this treatment for some time. After a while I had some quite adverse reactions to this medication. I had 12 hours of excruciating pain that felt like I was burning all over the skin of my body, arms, hands, legs, feet and face. I was taken off Betaferon, and put on Copaxone. While I was grateful for the new treatments, I still struggled with many MS symptoms.

One day I was hobbling along, aided by my two walking sticks. I had set out for a short walk. Well, suddenly fatigue hit me very hard. I was a long way from any bus stop. A bus driver saw me bent over on the side of the footpath, supported by my two walking sticks.

He stopped, and had mercy on me. He urged me to get on, as it was a busy time of the day. Then, I was dropped off near my home. You may be wondering why I was out at all, but to stay home all the time proved difficult. Another time I was staggering along, trying to get to the shops. I was zig-zagging, walking with difficulty from left to right. As I passed one man, he called out, "I want what you've got". I responded, "No you don't." He assumed I was on drugs.

Another day, I had an appointment with the Commonwealth Rehab Service at Rockdale in Sydney. They were trying to help me find work. I took my time getting to the train station. Then I got on the 'Tarago' – it was a Tangara train, but I always got the words mixed up with the Toyota mini-bus. I actually found a seat. Sometimes I had to stand with all my weight on the walking sticks, because of the weakness and pain in my legs, as all the seats were full. Other times I sat on the steps of the train, or on the floor. People like their seats. The train was also very warm and humid. It was winter and the air conditioning fully heated the train. This affected me, increasing my confusion and making me physically weaker and fatigued.

The train arrived at Rockdale, about a 20-minute ride all up. I stepped off the train, but in a very confused state of mind. I was unsure where I was and what I was supposed to be doing. Disorientated, I wandered around the platform, then, I walked toward the tracks. On the edge of the platform, the station guard came over and then guided me to the nearest seat. He wanted to call an ambulance, but upon my urging, chose not to. I sat there for 20 minutes in the cold, which cooled down my overheated body, then slowly walked to my appointment.

It may not need saying, but I was not really well enough to work. "De-nial, they say, is not just a river in Egypt." My doctor's secretary told me this. I was suffering from denial and spent many days pursuing work that I was not really up to doing. There was a reluctance in me to believe I had this disease, even with all the awful stuff that was happening to me. After all, I tried to convince myself, I was intelligent. I had been a teacher, a tradesman, a Youth Worker and had done three Diplomas and a Graduate Diploma. But the memory of them was fading fast as the MS ate away at my brain—so to speak. And I had great difficulty remembering information.

Another way MS affects me is that I am unable to regulate temperature changes within my body caused by environmental conditions. In the early days of my struggle with MS, I would walk into a warm (or cool) air-conditioned room, and just collapse, due to the sudden temperature change. I was invited by the MS Society to a Keep Fit water aerobics class at Sutherland Recreational Centre. Well, the class was held in an indoor heated pool. After about 20 minutes into the class, I heard someone call, "Stephen, get out of the pool!" I was completely confused and was sinking. The high humidity, breathing the humid, chlorinated air, and the warmth had caused me to become mentally confused and I almost passed out. That was the end of that. I was becoming quite afraid at this time. Where was this MS headed?

Chapter 4:

New Directions

I had a dream one night that I continue to think about. I was on a bushy mountain top with Richelle, and two children (even though we don't have children). I had my two walking sticks and was struggling to move. In the dream the Lord called me. I turned away from Richelle and walked towards the edge of a cliff top overlooking the Jamieson Valley (located in the Blue Mountains west of Sydney). The Lord God said, "Go to a man in the valley and tell him the good news of Jesus Christ!" It was about two kilometres down to the man's house far below, which I could not see from where I was, since I was so high up on the mountain. I wondered how I would get there.

In the dream, I then took one step off the edge of the cliff. Suddenly the power of God engulfed me and the Lord carried me down through the trees. I could feel the leaves of the trees brushing on my face, and the cold breeze blowing on me. I arrived at an old dirt road. There was dense bush everywhere and I saw a gate. I stood and called out to the man. He came out cursing. "Leave me alone!" Then he swore a lot. I told him of Jesus Christ and his love for sinners. He said he was not interested and swore some more. Then he asked me how I got to his totally 'inaccessible' place because he saw I had two walking sticks. I turned and pointed to the place I had come from, high up on the cliff face. He could not believe it. Then he surrendered to Jesus Christ and prayed.

Suddenly the Lord whisked me away. He lifted me just off the road and sped me away to another place. This time, in the same dream, I saw a large open field with a river going through it. There were many people getting baptized in this river. Geoff, a minister friend of mine, was doing the baptisms. The Lord said to me, "Go and pray for them (the baptized Christians) to receive the Holy Spirit." So, I obeyed. After this, I saw some people from my church, who were walking around and talking to each other. The Lord said, "Don't worry about them. Go!" Again, I started to walk, aided by my two sticks. In front of me was a zig-zag path that went up the mountain with many, many turns. I felt a moment of frustration that it was going to take a long time to walk up the mountain and get back to Richelle. It was surely an impossible task for me on my two walking sticks to think I could get back that way. Then I woke up from the dream. I was completely bathed with God's presence and His awesome love.

I often think about this dream. I believe it means that despite having MS and all the challenges it brings to my life, God has a plan for me and I can serve him anyway. I felt God's power in the dream and that something new was about to happen in my life. But it wasn't going to be easy.

Prayer Ministry

For quite some time after this I was very depressed. Gloom was all about me, with the severity of the MS attacks. I was seeing a Psychologist at the MS Society at Kogarah for counselling. This was because of continuing chronic pain, clinical depression and chronic anxiety.

Around this time, I started to really react to the Senior Pastor in my church. I said some bad things about him to others. Later, I realised this was slander. In James 5:16 it says, "Confess your sins to each other and pray for each other so that you may be healed. The prayer of a righteous person is powerful and effective." (NIV). I went to the pastor before a service and confessed my sin and sought his forgiveness. This was very hard for me to do, but he forgave me. The morning after confessing to my minister, God filled me with joy and the power of the Holy Spirit. I woke up praying in other languages and blessing God for His amazing love.

An elder in my church and friend of our family, Jean Williams said, "It is possible in the church to so plan that you actually plan God out of everything!" At the time our church was planning a lot of things and her concern was they weren't being bathed in prayer. Around this time another elder in our church, Mercia

Dellow, a prayer warrior and intercessor, went to be with Jesus (around July, 1998). To replace her, God raised up a few intercessors, that is, Christians to stand between God and his people and devote themselves to continuous prayer for local and world-wide issues. After I confessed slander, God called me to this new prayer ministry, for His glory and honour. A group of four or five from church met weekly to pray and intercede for our church, for Australia and for the world. We saw answers to prayer each time we met.

Jean was the one who also said to me, "Maybe the cross that you have to carry, Stephen, is MS." These were difficult words. Our Lord Jesus said, "Take up your cross and follow me." A cross for the Christian is a sign of dying to one's own desires, and following Christ's way each day. I was seeking Jesus and following God with all my heart. But the path that He had me take was not easy. This was just like my dream.

The early church, prayed and fasted, and prayed some more. During this period, I didn't watch television for two years, which was a kind of fast. God did some amazing things. One day I stood before the Lord in my room with my hands lifted up to God in prayer. A deep reverence came over me, because I knew I was in the presence of the Lord. I could not say a thing, but simply worshipped Him in fear and awe.

Another time, I was fasting and praying for people around the globe and in Australia to come to know Jesus Christ. God gave me opportunities to see things in the Spirit, with the clarity of a 4K TV! God gave me a vision of Australia. The country looked like it does on a map, but it was completely black. There was darkness all over the country, especially along the coast. However, there were little glimmers of light, which represented the churches. The Spirit of Jesus led me to pray for the many different nations and people groups that have come to this country. The Lord God moved me to pray for his church, along with binding the evil one. With and through the Holy Spirit, I used different bible verses to pray that the Lord would protect those who are His children. The blood of Jesus Christ was shed upon the cross. It demonstrates forgiveness for the sinner and complete cleansing from sin for those who believe in Jesus' death and resurrection. My prayers continued for God's church to be free from idolatry and divisions that have been such a poor witness to non-churched people. I asked for the Holy Spirit to come. I was praying for a public demonstration of the power of God. I was also meditating on Psalm 27, where God says, "Seek My face."

One time there was a flood in Africa and God called me to prayer. I saw the water draining from the surface of the earth. It actually happened and the flood cleared quickly. Another time, I was praying when I saw a group of Christians in a village in Africa with darkness hovering over them. Suddenly the power of God came over me and I bound Satan in the name of Jesus. The darkness fled and the people praised God. The things I saw and dreamed guided my prayers. I believe God was leading me about how to pray effectively. Even though I struggled with my physical health, God blessed me with encouraging experiences and answers to prayer.

I was so moved to pray that I contacted many local churches to try and establish a combined prayer ministry. The only ones who responded were the Catholics, who invited me to join their existing prayer group, which I did. They loved Jesus and expected His Spirit to move. One day I went to the prayer group and a lady started saying exactly what I had said privately to the Lord in prayer an hour before. This was word of knowledge and I was speechless. They advised me to quietly let the Lord minister to me. This was an enriching experience.

I noticed I became very angry with people close to me from mid 1998 to January 1999. I was hitting the wall in anger and sometimes even swearing. I did not realise it at this stage, but I was grieving. I had lost a lot and was in great turmoil within myself at this time, tormented in my mind, my spirit, and my being. This had been going on for two years, and was to last for two more. I was talking fast and quite distressed within myself. I wrote the poem below to express my intense feelings.

GRIEF

Stephen Hatton, 29th January, 1999

I lash out at you—because ...
There is no reason, or so it seems.
No cause for alarm, no condemnation meant,
As if I intended to cut you down.
To you I seem an enemy, a lost soul, a lost cause.

In the dark, in the day, whenever I cry
Tears may flow, I don't know why.
My heart is hard, a bit on the rough.
To listen to me, you'd think I'm tough.
But I am a boy in a big man's suit.

Deep down inside there's grief in them bones.
This man is crying out. To whom? Only God knows.
It's a terrible loss, the doctors all say,
To lose brain function and decision-making,
To learn, remember, make sense of the words.

I bash myself in anger, I curse, lash out. Failure! I'm a
failure.
Four diplomas, ten wasted years. I hardly remember
any of this training.
A trade, a Dip. Divinity and Mission, Dip. Teaching,
Grad. Dip. Computing, Dip. Business
All thrown out from this bloody disease!

You know, the doctor said it's OK to grieve. Not you,
it's the disease.

Your worth is that you're you, not defined by what you do.
MS sucks, I've always said. But MS is stuffed—I'd rather it dead!
I hate the thing inside my head—a cursed disease eating my nerves.
The threat of eye loss, fatigue, weakness, shaking, spasms ... Ah!

O God, lay Your healing hand upon this aching soul.
Please, dear Jesus Christ, I ask You to make me whole.
Less pain at this point, proof of Your hand. A more peaceful outlook.
Keep me at peace with those I love, myself and You, Lord above.

You know me as Stephen, Oh Lord of all creation.
I am here for these short years, while you are eternal, forever near,
Choosing to be one with us through Christ Your Son.
I feel my lack of self respect, of feeling peace within.

You love me dearly, as the death of Jesus on Calvary shows.
Bless You, Lord God! All thanks to your Name.
You are my Saviour, my life, my all –
Worthy of Honour, all glory and praise. Amen!

In church one morning, while prayers were being said, I screamed out in pain. A lightning bolt went through my whole body. Another time I hobbled into church with my two walking sticks. My legs went numb, and I had to be carried out. Other people were very distressed for me at that time. It was three hours before the feeling came back. All this was part of the struggle I had with MS.

Two close friends of mine urged me to go to the healing service at St Andrews Cathedral in Sydney at 6pm one Wednesday night. I went with Richelle. I listened to the talk. Afterwards they invited people who wanted prayer to put their hands up. Two ladies, one quite poor, the other with much gold jewellery on, prayed for me in the mighty name of Jesus. I don't remember what they said. However, I walked out with little pain and no sense of depression at all. God does answer prayer. After suffering for so many years, I am so grateful to God for those women and their prayers.

A Vision

I was lying down, when I felt an urgency to pray in the Spirit. God said, "I Am going to take you through a time of darkness when you will not see Me or know Me." Before me was a gentle slope that represented six years of severe suffering with MS for both me and my wife as my carer. Suddenly, it dropped into utter darkness. My heart sank. Then God said, "You won't see me in the darkness but I will bring you into a green pasture." A line went almost vertically straight up to a really beautiful green pasture with the sun shining brightly on it. This was around April 2001. I wondered what this meant.

A friend asked me to visit his church in Canberra to see an elder who had prayed for a sick person and seen a cure. He thought this man could pray for me. As they were praying, His Pastor said to me, "I'm not praying for your healing, but rather that God will achieve everything He wants to through your life, no matter what that may be." That was a difficult prayer and not exactly what I wanted to hear! From this time on, I prayed as follows. "Lord, your will be done," and "You are writing the story." I was seeking God with my whole heart, soul and mind, giving Him reverence and honour and time, of which I had a lot! This was in May 2001.

My periods of fasting went from missing lunch here and there to whole days. Then came one whole week of earnestly seeking Jesus Christ, without water, drink, or food. All I wanted at that time was to have an intimate relationship with God, as our Lord Jesus Christ did with God His Father and the Holy Spirit here on earth, (recorded for us in John 17:20-23). I was praying, meditating on, and devouring scripture too. As well, I was praying for the church and myself. In the words of Paul, "I keep asking that the God of our Lord Jesus Christ, the glorious Father, give you the Spirit of wisdom and revelation, so that you may know Him better." (Ephesians 1:17). As you can see, I was neglecting others, including my wife. I was consumed with the pursuit of God. I recognise now that I was on the way to becoming mentally unwell, but I didn't have insight at the time.

Through God, I believe I started prophesying, in church and in public places. One day, I struggled to walk into my home church aided by my two walking sticks. It was such an effort to walk. Richelle and I went to a meeting of our whole church with an architect, Ridley Smith, to discuss the new church building plan. I was sitting there when a strong impression came into my mind. "Hear O Israel, the Lord, our God, the Lord is one. You shall love the Lord your God." At that point I asked God in my mind, if it was the Lord, would he give me courage to speak. Suddenly my lungs filled with his Holy Spirit. I shot to my feet (without walking sticks) and spoke these words. "Hear O Israel, the Lord our God, the Lord is One. You shall love the Lord your God with all your heart, and all your soul, and with all your mind, and all your strength. What kind of temple will you build for me? Or where will my dwelling place be? The Heavens, the highest heavens cannot contain me..." There was more but I don't remember what it was. I sat down and the whole seat was vibrating, I felt as if I was under God's awesome power. To God be the Glory! Great things He has done for His purpose. When this happened, I became truly terrified of the power of the Living God.

About this time Michael Cassidy from African Enterprise came to speak to our church at Miranda function rooms. I was very ill with MS all throughout this time. I felt sick from the constant fatigue and pain in my body, and I was quite nauseated. After his message, Michael called for people to come forward and give their lives to God in mission. As people were going forward, Richelle went too. Suddenly the Lord said, "Stand up and testify." I asked Richelle to help me get up. Michael asked me what I was doing there, with my two walking sticks. I told him what the Lord had said. He said not to say anything yet. He spoke and prayed, then holding me with one hand and Richelle with the other, Michael said that now was the time. The power of God consumed me and I prophesied, "Seek my face." There was more, but I have no recollection of it. People helped me to my seat, and Jean, the lady from our church already identified, prayed over me in the Spirit, and I became calm. The power of God is truly awesome.

Chapter 5:

The Dive into Utter Darkness

There was much distress in me at this time. My thoughts were perseverating, that is going round and around all the time. I was still fasting. I was very unsettled, speaking in tongues a lot, sometimes with interpretation. Somewhere in there, I felt like someone started pushing me along. Driven along by an unseen force, I went to our local shopping centre, Miranda Fair, shouting out the words, "All men are like grass and all their glory is like the flowers of the field. The grass withers, the flowers fall, but the word of the Lord stands forever." (1 Peter 1:24-25).

I was at my parents-in-law for a family get-together, on Mothers' Day in 2001. I stood up and told everyone I was going to Africa to tell people about Jesus. This was all in response to a dream I had. I'd seen a jumbo jet, a ship, and a large area filled with people ready to hear about Jesus. My family were confused and becoming very worried about me. My mind was playing tricks on me, and I did not perceive it. I was so unwell with MS. I was using two walking sticks still to keep me upright because I was so weak. It was a very difficult time. Needless to say I did not go to Africa.

Often the Lord would say to my spirit, "Be still and know that I am God!" (See Psalm 46:10.) I would fall face down at His feet. The Bible says that God's strength (power) is made perfect in weakness. (II Corinthians 12:9.) I was at the weakest point in my life mentally, spiritually, physically and emotionally. I had sought the Lord with all my heart, soul, mind, and strength. I did not have anything left. I was totally spent.

I started having terrible dreams and visions of the judgment time. In one dream I saw an Angel. It was very tall and immense in stature. The angel had one foot in one country, and the other foot in another country, divided by sea. It was beaming like the sun! In another dream, I gave a large amount of money, $50,000, to God for his use. I saw thousands of angels in the atmosphere above the world, moving about like lightning around a throne. Immediately upon giving the money to the church, the angels moved very quickly to the earth, to our church, and Revival broke out.

Things came to a head when Richelle and I stayed up all night at my insistence, waiting for a blessing from God in the form of a delivery, which never came. The next morning, I urged Richelle to stay home from work, as God was going to speak to us. Richelle was very worried and rang my parents. She didn't know what to do. My mother came over and sat with Richelle. She realised I needed help and contacted the Mental Health Team at Sutherland Hospital. They agreed to send a team over but could not say when. It was about lunch time when she rang and they did not arrive until 9pm that night. I was unaware of all this at the time due to what I was experiencing.

I was wide awake when I saw a vision, a picture in the air, like watching TV. I saw a very long, wide conveyor belt. I was in the middle of this conveyor belt, and four black Panthers were on each corner. I was in space, and it was pitch black and very dark. I was very scared. I was on the conveyor belt for some time slowly moving along. Then there appeared to the left of me a gigantic Lion. I was tiny like an ant in comparison. The face of the Lion was huge and very golden in colour. Beside the Lion on each side, were two very large Spirit forms. One represented the Son, and the other, the Holy Spirit. I was trembling with fear.

As the conveyor belt went past the beings, I suddenly turned around and cursed God, accusing the Holy Spirit of being evil. God the Father rose and said, "Depart from me into the eternal fire prepared for the Devil and his angels!" In a split second, an angel grabbed me by the shoulders and threw me into a massive fiery place burning with unquenchable fire. Satan, looking like a serpent, was burning too, writhing in agony. The flames reached very high into space. I screamed out and collapsed. I felt my spirit ripped out of me at that very moment. I was terrified and petrified. I went into a catatonic state. I was so terrified, my body and mind shut down. I couldn't talk or respond or think.

Richelle came to me and tried to talk with me. I could barely hear her, as I was in a state of sheer terror. God had departed from me. My teeth were clenched, and I could still see the flames. My parents came to talk as well, but I could not reply. Then, Sutherland Hospital Mental Health team came. I could not talk to them either. A voice spoke to me. "If you say anything, all your loved ones will burn up in front of you too." I was totally lost. The mental health team gave Richelle some medicine to give to me. They agreed I needed to go to hospital but there were no beds available. So, they left, and my parents left, and we were left alone.

Mental Illness

The next day, I went to the hospital in an ambulance. At the hospital I got off the trolley and fell prostrate before God on the ground. The wardens came and asked who put me there. I can remember these things, but I could not do a thing about them. I was admitted to hospital.

Later, my psychiatrist said to me, "It's not your fault". These words meant a lot to me at the time, though I could not fully process them. She said the visions and dreams were of my hopes and fears. I was in a catatonic state. That is the worst form of mental breakdown you can have. She said that if they had not got me at that time, I would have died. They restarted my brain with a number of bouts of electro-convulsive therapy, an electric current into the brain. I only needed a few treatments, but I suffered memory loss due as a result. This period was traumatic for Richelle, our parents, and our families.

I was in hospital for two weeks. People assumed I was hospitalised because of my MS and in a way this was true. I was diagnosed with schizophrenia secondary to MS, meaning the MS caused the mental illness. The family did not tell anyone outside the family about my mental illness. At the time, it was considered shameful and not talked about. I'm glad things have changed. I was put on medication to help control the illness.

My sister Christine said, "Maybe you've had a taste of what Jesus went through." My other sister Michelle commented, "This is a crisis of faith for Stephen." For me at the time, it was sheer hell. I felt my spirit ripped out! Where was God in this suffering? Did he cause it? There were so many questions and there seemed to be no answers. When I got home from hospital I was in a state of spiritual distress. I still did not know where God had gone. There was no peace, only turmoil and always the memory of the flames and torment I had been through. I felt like I had been gutted.

At this time a lady rang me, doing a survey on movies on the phone. I cried into the phone saying, "I don't know whether I'm a Christian or not." She replied, "What do you know?"

I said I knew that Jesus died on the cross, but I was numb saying these words. Then she stated with conviction, "Jesus rose from the dead!" She said she did not want to lose her job, so she would call me next week.

I got off the phone, and opened my Bible to 1 Peter 1:3-7. "All praise to God the Father of our Lord Jesus Christ. It is by his mercy that we have been born again, because God raised Jesus Christ from the dead. Now we live with great expectation, and we have a priceless inheritance - an inheritance that is kept in heaven for you, pure and undefiled, beyond the reach of change and decay. And through your faith God is protecting you by His power, until you receive this salvation, which is ready to be revealed on the last day for all to see". (New Living Translation). The lady rang a week later, true to her word. She was a Christian and a pastor. We had several conversations and she tried to encourage me.

But by this time, I had decided enough was enough. I wanted to end it all. I was going to take my life. I couldn't cope anymore.

The Green Pasture

The next morning, after I got up, I suddenly had a vision. There was a vivid picture in front of me of three small steps going up to a green pasture. The sun shone brightly on the field of rich green grass which went on forever, no matter where I looked. Suddenly, a peace from God flooded my whole being, along with a sense of freedom from all the intense suffering I had been through. I was swamped by God's peace. For three weeks God bathed me in this peace. I could hardly speak either. Then I went to see a Star Wars movie (bad move) and the intense peace left. But there was a stillness in me, a quiet calm. It became evident to everyone who knew of the torment I had been through that a significant change had occurred in me. I went from very distressed, distraught and driven along, to a calm state of mind, quite at peace.

This vision was the culmination of the earlier vision I'd had. I now understood the earlier vision was a warning of what was to come. I really did go down into the darkness as the vision showed me. But now I was coming out the other side and finally going into the green pasture.

After church one morning, a Christian brother Clint, walked up to me and said through the Spirit of God, "There is no condemnation in Christ Jesus, our Lord." (Romans 8, verse 1) The scary vision with fire made me feel judged and condemned to an eternity without

Jesus and without hope. This verse was another aspect to the healing God was bringing to me. I wept and wept because it was the first time someone said something positive to me. Clint did not know what I had been through. But God did and so did I! I felt a glimmer of hope.

A few years later, Michael Cassidy, head of African Enterprise, came to our church again. He confirmed that my prophecy from his last visit at Miranda was God's doing. This meant a lot to me. I had begun to think it was all psychosis or mental illness. He urged me to seek God with all my heart. He prayed for an open door to health. Michael took me aside after church. He said, by God's Spirit, "I know the plans I have for you, declares the Lord: plans to prosper you and not to harm you; plans to give you hope and a future." (Jeremiah 29:11-12). At first, I did not take it to heart. However, Richelle said to me at home later that day, "God is not out to harm you. He is not out to get you." Something inside me broke. I wept uncontrollably for a long time. Richelle tried to console me, but couldn't. The grief I had bottled up was finally being released.

I was so upset as a result of that vision I had of God condemning me to hell, and seeing the flames. I did not understand so many things. I felt God was out to get me and I blamed Him for giving me the vision. I had been seeking the Lord Jesus with all my heart, when the vision occurred. I did not eat or drink for 5 days before the vision. I was so keen to have an intimate relationship with God, just as Jesus Christ did with his Father and the Holy Spirit. As I reflect, I remember praying for a public demonstration of the Holy Spirit too. Yes, this did happen a number of times, in church and in public places. But I was also unwell too at this time, because of the MS, a lack of food, and other things that were scrambling my brain.

Through the week of fasting and great distress I had been through, I did lose a lot of weight.

I weighed only 76 kilograms. I had been 84 kgs for the three years previously. (One year later, I was to reach 109 kgs after taking certain psychiatric medications!)

To hear the words read from the Bible, 'Be still and know that I am God,' would cause me to collapse in fear. Or, if they were sung in a Christian song, the same response would happen, even in church. I had become very afraid of God. Post Traumatic Stress Disorder had set in. A Senior Clinical Psychologist at the MS Society counselled me for anxiety and pain management during this period.

1 Peter 1:6 states, "Though now for a little while, you may have had to suffer grief in all kinds of trials. These have come so that your faith, – of greater worth than gold…- may be proved genuine and may result in praise, glory and honour when Jesus Christ is revealed."

Hebrews 12:10-11 says, "But God disciplines us for our good, that we may share in His holiness. No discipline seems pleasant at the time, but painful. Later on, however, it produces a harvest of righteousness and peace, for those who have been trained by it." (NIV)

However, I will say now that God has brought good out of this awful time. His peace is in my mind and heart –not the same intensity as for the first three weeks after the suffering, but an enduring calm in my soul, a sense of freedom from having to do things to please God, which really mattered to me. Another verse which has come to mean a lot to me is this one from Romans 14:17, "The Kingdom of God is not a matter of food and drink, but of righteousness, peace and joy in the Holy Spirit." God is with me again.

Chapter 6:

Moving Forward

After suffering for so many years, God met me again through the Ministry at St.Andrew's Cathedral. After a couple of believers prayed, I was encouraged to go to the front to be anointed with oil. Then I was prayed over by the elders believing in my healing in Jesus' Name. This happened many times over about 12 years. As I was so sick, it was difficult to believe this for myself. Thank God others did.

We also went to St Mary's Christian Life Church, (a place in western Sydney), where my sister Michelle was baptized. I was struggling with my two walking sticks. Richelle was by my side, and my dear parents as well. At the end of the service, the whole church waited on God. I had never seen anything like it. Music played softly and the church was quiet. Then one by one people came up the front to testify to God healing them. Some were instantly healed of cancer. I thought, "What about me?" I was very self-focused and quite angry at missing out. I seemed to be the only one who really looked sick.

Forgiving the Unforgivable

For two separate years, I went to a Chronic Illness workshop at Golden Grove in Newtown, Sydney. It is part of the St Andrew's Cathedral Healing Ministry. Canon Holbeck taught that just as Jesus Christ had forgiven all those who came to Him, so we ought to forgive, completely and without resentment, those who have sinned against us. As I see it, that means those who have done and said things that hurt me as well. Jesus said, "Forgive, as I have forgiven you."

Well, this is the way it happened for me. I hadn't been able to forgive some people. I felt really hurt, harbouring deep resentment and bitterness towards both a former employer and a minister. We were urged to write what had happened to us on a piece of paper, then throw it into a bucket that was then set on fire. I came to forgive them, without regret, in Jesus' Name. About a month later, something amazing happened. God gave me my legs back. The pain and weakness left, and eventually, so did the walking sticks. Day by day my legs became stronger. I had to learn to walk again with confidence. I had become so attached to these supports through years of use. So, God's people prayed and prayed, and the Lord did this physical healing, to His Glory. Sometime later, I noticed that another quiet miracle had occurred. The severe and debilitating fatigue left too. Hallelujah!

Tysabri Infusions

For 22 years, I continued to travel to Liverpool Hospital, in order to see my specialist and have treatment in the Ambulatory Care ward. (Liverpool is 45 minutes' drive north-west from our home in Gymea.) They are truly wonderful people. Nurses and other staff are very caring. There are three important things to share about the new medicine my MS specialist neurologist had now recommended for me, which works to remyelinate the nerves.

1. On the website was a warning—This drug can cause irreversible brain disease.

2. Tysabri was not available on the Pharmaceutical Benefits Scheme (PBS), which provides government subsidies for medication. It was going to cost $3000 for each 30ml treatment. I prayed about this as we could not afford it. Friends and family came forward and offered to kindly contribute to the costs of these treatments. My Mum and Dad, Tina and Rod, and Aunty Anne and Uncle Ray, meaning we only paid for one treatment ourselves. I am forever grateful to these wonderfully generous people. I had four infusions before it was approved for inclusion in the PBS reducing the cost to $45 per dose.

3. Before going onto Tysabri, I usually had about four good health days per month.

A friend helped me accept this new medication, in spite of the frightening warning. He had suffered immensely with a bone marrow transplant. He was able to persuade me to accept the risks in the light of the benefits. I was very afraid of any possible brain disease.

After about 18 infusions (via a vein in my arm,) I was having around 26 good health days per month. This was the case for two years. Then, for some unknown reason, I went to about 16 good health days per month. The specialist discovered that I had the JC Virus antibody, which can cause brain disease, so the treatment was stopped.

Opportunities and Stories

I have had countless opportunities to tell my story to people. Sometimes I will be waiting at the bus stop, and someone will recognize me as the man who used to walk with the aid of not one, but two, walking sticks! Or it would happen during my visits to hospital.

My wife and I were in Queenstown, New Zealand on an overseas holiday. We packed up after a wonderful trip full of adventure. As we arrived at the airport, there was thick cloud all over the place. An Airbus flew overhead. We passengers soon discovered that that was our plane flying to Sydney, without us on it. Anyone who has been to Queenstown knows that the airport is situated between two towering mountains, the runway is very short and narrow, and impossible to land on when the cloud base is low. A lady came out and informed the passengers that they had to make their own way home, or catch an eight hour bus trip to Christchurch. Stress and anxiety were visible on the faces of most passengers.

I was in a hyper-anxious state myself, as I was on a particular dose of Risperdal that made me anxious and highly agitated. But I felt compelled to pray earnestly to God, asking that the thick cloud might clear, and that He would give wisdom to the airways staff. I asked it all in the Name of Jesus. God Almighty answered that prayer. A short time later, the cloud began to lift and a jet was able to land. We were not flown home to Sydney, but were flown to Christchurch. We had an extra day as a bonus in New Zealand before flying home via Auckland. God is so good.

Some verses that have encouraged me to pray believing God for the impossible are the words of Jesus Christ our Lord. He said, "I will do whatever you ask for in My name, so that the Son may bring glory to the Father. You may ask for anything in my name and I will do it." John 14:13 and 15:7. As well, Paul writes in 2 Thessalonians 1:11-12, "With this in mind we constantly pray for you, that our God may count you worthy of His calling, and that by His power he may fulfil every good purpose of yours and every act prompted by your faith. We pray this so that the name of our Lord Jesus may be glorified in you and you in Him, according to the grace of our God and the Lord Jesus Christ."

As far as getting back into paid work goes, I was referred to the Salvation Army Work Support Centre in 2008 for an assessment. After going there for two weeks, this is roughly what was said: "Stephen, we have 24 work placement centres. However, you are not eligible for work as you cannot cope with air conditioning, and you get so confused." Air conditioning was a challenge because the quick changes in temperature were too much for me to cope with. They would lead to me collapsing and being fatigued. Life is indeed complex.

I went to a speech therapist around this time, because I was often not understood, due to my mixed-up speech and jumbled words. She said to try describing something that is similar to the word or phrase you're trying to say. One day I went to the chemist to get a script filled.

I said to Mr Robinson, "I ampt!" He said, "Go home and have a sleep!" Some words I've found similar when I can't find just the right one are illustrated in what follows.

Richelle and I were to go out. It was pouring with rain. I could not find 'it' anywhere. "Where is my raindrop remover?" I asked her. It was of course an umbrella. I'd often say to Richelle, "Can you go to the white box in the kitchen?" She'd spend five minutes trying to decipher what I was talking about. That's right, it was the fridge! Another time, I was at my friend Jason's funeral. All was quiet, as the occasion demanded. Suddenly I burst into laughter. I was recalling to myself the events of that morning. I had ironed my face and shaved my clothes. Of course, it was the other way round. Thankfully, other people were very understanding.

Increasingly, I continue to have trouble processing information. The challenge is to find relevant information when asked a question. I either go blank, or I just need to spend a few minutes fishing for the right words. I have great difficulty finding a reference point in my mind in order to answer someone else's question. The way MS continues to affect me is still located in my brain, due to damaged nerve pathways. I really do continue to have difficulty with thinking and processing information, as well as comprehension and cognition.

Brother Yun, the Heavenly Man, a Chinese Christian, came to speak at Southside Church in Sydney. His Chinese-to-English interpreter called people to the front for prayer. As the interpreter came around praying for people, he said to me, "I have a word from God for you. "Although the Lord gives you the bread of adversity and the water of affliction, your teachers will be hidden no more. With your own eyes you will see them. Your ears will hear a voice behind you saying, 'This is the way: walk in it.'" (Isaiah 30:20-21).

Since then, the Holy Spirit has impressed upon me to believe in surrender. God is awesome in His work. These words encourage me and are in the Scriptures. "Be strong in the Lord and His mighty power." (Ephesians 6:10). "Seek the Lord while he may be found." (Isaiah 55:6). "Trust in the Lord with all your heart." (Proverbs 3:5). "Be strong and courageous. Do not be afraid; do not be discouraged, for the Lord your God will be with you wherever you go." (Joshua 1: 9). "Cast your cares on the Lord, for he cares for you." (1 Peter 5:7). "Seek my face." (Psalm 27:8). These words really encourage me. God truly is so very good. In the midst of my suffering and turmoil, God has met me and brought His Word to my mind.

Chapter 7:

Acceptance and Healing

In May 2010, one of my specialists said that the psychosis – the mental illness, including the visions and dreams that I suffered in 2001—could have been a consequence of the Methyl Prednisone treatment. Another specialist believed it was an MS attack. Whatever, it sucks! I am not sure that it brings me any closer to closure. I just have to accept the way things are, without constantly seeking to understand. Acceptance brings peace.

Playing electric guitar in church had been a real blessing to me, and to others, however, now I can only partially see the music. At other times, I cannot make sense of the chord patterns or even remember them. So I have now stepped down from this role, a real disappointment at the time but now I've made my peace with it.

I have been very anxious for a long time. Since my HECS (Higher Education Contribution Scheme) debt started in 1991, I have been unable to pay back the $2000 owed for my Teacher Training. My GP at the time wrote a supportive letter in 1995, asking for it to be cancelled. It wasn't. My dad wrote a superb letter to our Federal Representative in 2004, and I was commended for my studies by the Minister for Education. He explained the debt stands, and will be cancelled at my death. Meanwhile it continues to accumulate every year. I have been very stressed at times about this issue. So, I finally wrote a letter myself to the Prime Minister of Australia, asking for the debt to be cancelled, and I sent it off. But the slate wasn't wiped clean. I'll still have to pay it back, if ever I earn a substantial income, which in all honesty is unlikely. The good outcome from all this was that after I sent my final letter, I prayed to God Most High and I forgave the Government for my HECS debt. Healing comes through forgiveness. I have been at peace about it ever since. That was in March 2010. God is so good! I know they will not cancel the debt, but it no longer matters to me. God has dealt with my heart.

On 29 November, 2010, Richelle and I sent this email to many people in our worldwide network.

Dear Family, Friends, and Brothers and Sisters in the Lord Jesus Christ.

I have very good news. God is continuing to heal me on the inside, and on the outside. Recently I was set free from fear. This fear was because of some graphic visions of Hell, which I had in 2001. These have kept me afraid of meeting God in the judgement, and very anxious for nine years.

Some time back, our Minister, Pastor Graham, talked to me and walked me through some of the Son of God's promises in the Christian Bible. (See John 10:27-30 and Romans 8:28-30) Basically, Jesus says ... if I turn my life over to Him, I have eternal life, and I will never perish. No one can snatch me out of His hands. And no one can snatch me out of the Father's hands. And Jesus said, I and the Father are One. He is God. It was as though I had heard this clearly for the first time. God opened my ears to hear and to receive this amazing truth. He set me free! I feel alive inside and very well.

Thank you for your enduring prayers, filled with hope and faith, for the good things God has for Richelle and me. All things really are possible with Him. He has set me free to seek Jesus with all my heart and mind and to proclaim Him. (Psalm 105:1-4)

I was disabled, now I walk. I was in severe pain, now I laugh. I was in despair, now I have hope. My brain was scrambled, now I think relatively clearly. I was dying inside for over 8 years, now I am alive. I was afraid, bound by fear and anxiety, now I am free! Thank you, Lord Jesus. How awesome is the Most High. Through God's power, and with the help of 35 Tysabri Infusions (so far) and your prayers, I am a walking miracle. It is truly amazing to me what God has done—I feel like a new person with a new lease of life. Many others who have known me keep telling me about the change they see in me: e.g. the Chemist, hospital staff, Doctors, friends, family and my dear Richelle. God has answered so many of my prayers, many of which were prayed with anger, great grief and tears over 16 years. I have been crying from joy lately. I am absolutely overwhelmed at God's grace to me, including the stillness and peace of God inside me.

MS is still there, showing up when I least expect it. But I keep my eyes on Jesus. I was diagnosed in January 1994—16 years ago. It is 15 years since I have worked for any income. Now, God is leading me in a fresh new way. One of the verses that has most helped me through life with the monster MS is "Cast (throw) all your anxiety (anything troubling you) on the Lord Jesus, for He cares for you. (1Peter 5:7)

PS: I am also writing an account of my journey dealing with this monster, Multiple Sclerosis, and my relationship with Jesus Christ throughout this time. Maybe I'll finish it next year. In my spare time, I am painting, writing songs, making furniture, and mostly enjoying life with Richelle.

Someone once said to me, "The best things in life are not things". This is true. I can see now that genuine relationships with people are far more important than material objects. The more I visit God's people, the more I am deeply moved by his love and power working in them to make us more like Jesus. And, the more I look forward to seeing our Lord Jesus Christ in person. How awesome will it be when He comes again!

All our love in Jesus' Name,
Stephen and Richelle

I received the following response to this letter from Michael Cassidy.

You can't imagine how blessed and encouraged I've been by your letters. It was just a joy and delight and a blessing to my spirit to get your good news after all these years and the extensive time lapse since we were last in touch. I remember numbers of our conversations so it was a blessing indeed to hear from you with this kind of good news. It's also an inspiration for me and anyone else hearing your testimony because it brings to us all afresh just how supernatural is our Lord and the things He does. So, thank you for this communication and may you go on from strength to strength. May the Lord's healing in you be complete, and may your joy continue to overflow. And may your testimony gain a wide hearing and touch many both in their physical bodies and in their inner souls.

And now may the Lord give to you and Richelle and your family a truly blessed Christmas and a new year filled to overflowing with His good things. And of course, you may definitely use episodes in which I was involved with you as you share your story in your book. And may the book gain a wide hearing and acceptance.

Do keep in touch.

Warmly in the love of Christ
Michael Cassidy

African Enterprise

At this stage, I could name about ten things that have happened, through which God has brought healing and wholeness to me that I can see—the truth is there may be a myriad of others.

• The consistent believing prayers of God's people over 17 years;

• St Andrew's Cathedral Healing Ministry, where I have been anointed with oil many   times as people prayed faith-filled prayers over me in Jesus Christ's Mighty Name;

• The Centre at Golden Grove in Newtown, where I have attended Workshops on forgiveness for bitterness and resentment toward others, and on grief and loss for not being able to have children;

• Many Tysabri Infusions under my excellent specialist and her team at Liverpool Hospital;

• Encouragement from the Scriptures and words of grace that people have spoken to me;

• My Psychiatrist's management of my mental health and psychotic episodes;

• Dr Gary Fulcher from the MS Society and his team for helping me with Post-traumatic Stress Disorder, chronic pain and anxiety;

- Our parents and family members, whose sustained support has been invaluable;

- My dear wife Richelle who has stood by me through everything, and whose patience
and grace is a reflection of her relationship with the living Lord Jesus Christ; and

- The Lord our God who has met me with His deliverance, peace and freedom.

At this time, I felt that I had finished my book and should get it published. I was also asking myself the question, "Can I work?" I have seen an opportunity to help people make informed decisions about buying televisions and products that go with them, before they go to a salesman in a retail shop. What I still don't know is how to get paid for this thoroughly researched information.

We had a Guidance sermon one Sunday, then as my wife and I walked back into our block of units, a local business woman met us, and said, "Stephen, you've got to go to this tomorrow. Sutherland Council and the Local Business Enterprise Centre are putting on a free program for Business Development Week." I did, and it proved to be thoroughly worthwhile taking part. At this time, I was well and very optimistic. I think I was buoyed by the hope that something new had opened up. My business was going to be called 'Digital4U'. But before
I could register it as a domain name, I became ill again, and someone else took the name.

Chapter 8:

Ch-Ch-Changes

In October 2012, I was still seeking God. But MS was the root cause of my problems at this time. Schizophrenia (secondary to MS) was the diagnosis. This is another form of psychosis.

In my deluded state, I sneakily stopped taking any sort of medicine, contributing to my poor health. I threw out a lot of things: my full business plan, all the backup disks, along with a USB drive; my wedding ring, because I thought it was all evil; some of my wife's important notes, and my electric guitar effects pedal board (very expensive, and thankfully my dad came and got it).

One morning I woke up well before my wife at 5am. I went to pray. A strong thought came into my head. "I, your Lord and commander, command you to go!" I was afraid, but thinking it was God, I left. No keys, no wallet, and I didn't tell Richelle, either. I walked for about 8 kilometres, then came home, distressed and afraid. Meanwhile, Richelle had gone looking for me, so I had to wait outside for her to return and let me in. I genuinely felt abandoned by God at this time. How could God let me go through another bout of mental illness, hearing God requiring me to do things which were out of my control?

My wife Richelle and I had made plans to go on a European Holiday. I was just too unwell to even cope with the possibility. In my psychotic state, I had become super anxious about everything. With my blessing, Richelle's Mum went with her so she didn't have to cancel the trip or go alone. At one point, she made a video call from Paris. At the time, my Dad and I were present. I was becoming very afraid of God's holiness and honour. But I was so fearful of God that I couldn't tell my wife that I loved her. Why was God allowing me to get psychotic, and so skewed, about Christian things?

After that event, there have been no more messages or visions—just absolute silence for the next ten years. I have found the slow recovery extremely difficult. My faith in God has been severely shaken.

My psychiatrist then put me on Saphris, an anti-psychotic medicine. This helped me immensely and kept the psychotic symptoms under control. It has become clear that I will have to continue on with psychiatric medication for life.

Back to disability

After 16 years of walking unaided after my healing in 2001, everything changed in a moment. In November 2017, everything fell apart. I was standing having a conversation with my Aunty Hope. Without warning, my legs gave way and I crashed to the ground. I found myself lying on the ground confused. This was the first of more than thirty falls which happened to me over the next three years. The doctors concluded that they were all MS-related incidents. The muscles in my legs holding me up simply switched off, due to faulty messages from my brain. I see this as an MS relapse – healthy one minute, smitten with multiple symptoms the next.

Then myoclonic jerks and spasms started happening. These are quick, involuntary muscular actions. I was in bed sound asleep when suddenly both legs kicked out, my arms flew up, my back arched, and my neck was thrown back. I thought my neck was going to break. This was very painful. All this took less than a second in time, as all my muscles went hard instantly with pain, then totally relaxed. After that shock to the system, I fell asleep. This became an ongoing issue and was the start of many hundreds of myclonic jerks. The bad ones compress my ribs to the centre of my sternum. Very painful!

I have also had MS seizures which were definitely not caused by epilepsy, as observed by my neurologist at the time via an EEG. The seizures are quite violent, shaking me. They only last for about 5 to 20 seconds, and I remain aware the whole time, and they completely debilitate me. My energy level goes from full on to nothing in seconds. My specialist put me on three different medicines to try and manage these symptoms. They did lessen the severity of the spasms but they did not resolve completely.

I had poor balance, and I had to go back to using 2 walking sticks, a walking frame, and from time to time using my electric scooter. We eventually realised that the medicines were contributing to me being so unwell, disabled again, very weak and continually fatigued so my doctor took me off them all. My disability level improved significantly and I was able to walk unaided again!

My specialist continues to explore all new medical developments. I have recently had the second dose of Mavenclad (Cladribine) – a relatively new MS treatment. Now I have not had to take anything for the last three years. I am now seeing a neurologist at St George Hospital, mainly because she's closer to my place and more accessible. My former specialist is so busy in her numerous diagnostic and research roles at Liverpool Hospital and the University of NSW.

Pastor Brook, from See Change Church in Jannali, was praying for me after church one day and said, "I see a Jenga block set, high and upright. Suddenly it smashed to the ground. Then each time a block is added, it crashes to the ground again." He didn't know me at that time, but that was exactly how I felt. Jenga is a game with wooden building blocks, the aim being to build as high as you can without the tower toppling over. This encouraged me greatly as it showed me God knows how I'm feeling.

Excruciating right leg pain off the Richter Scale started in 2020. The pain turns on all the nerves in my whole right leg at the same time, beyond my ability to cope. It only lasts a few seconds. My wife and my Mum and others prayed and there was no more pain for a while. Then it came back—once a week sometimes, a few times another week, then nothing for a fortnight. Very random, it just sneaks up on me. My physiotherapist says it's MS pain from a lesion in my spine or brain. It's not muscular or skeletal. After sitting for twenty minutes, the pain may or may not occur again—completely unpredictable. Sometimes I'm sound asleep, and I scream out in pain, awoken by a bolt of nerve electricity. Sometimes my wife and I laugh shortly after it, trying to make a joke to break the tension. One day the pain was about four times worse than usual and lasted for 30 seconds, turning into a sensation like my whole right leg was burning on fire. It's weird, ongoing and unpredictable. Unfortunately, this pain has continued to progress and intensify, sometimes occurring multiple times a day.

I am not receiving the Disability Support Pension, but I am a grateful recipient of the Australian Government's National Disability Insurance Scheme

(NDIS). I have received considerable professional and practical help. One area that has been invaluable is exercise physiology. I saw the person treating me at her practice. When I first went to her in 2018, I could barely stand. Now I walk everywhere confidently. She has helped me get stronger and fitter. I have had wonderful support workers, including two particular individuals who have worked with me for several years and who take me out into the community. Without them, I would be spending much of my time at home alone while Richelle goes to work. We would not have been able to afford to fund this ourselves, so the NDIS funding is a huge blessing and has improved my quality of life.

I also have a group of men who have been great supporters that I meet with for morning tea each Tuesday. They are my good friends the two Johns, Dave, Lloyd, and my dad Neville. This friendship group has also been invaluable to get me out and about.

I still feel really keen to work. So far I have advised at least twelve people regarding the choice and purchase of new televisions for the best price. I advise them what to buy, what to look for, features to get, and brands that are reliable. All of them have taken my advice and been happy with the outcome. This makes me feel valuable and encouraged that I can help others by making complex ideas simple.

In the last few years, I have had an important and significant dream, which encouraged me as well as helping me understand part of my life.

Black Snake Dream

15th August 2021

I had an incredible dream that had a scary start, but God transformed the ending beyond what I could think or imagine. In this dream I had a Holden LJ silver Torana, a car I had once owned, but which was written off by the insurance company when an out-of-control vehicle smashed into it. I dreamt I was in the back seat when I saw a red-bellied black snake (quite a poisonous Australian snake) more than a metre in length on the floor below my feet. It was menacing. I tried to catch it but couldn't. I tried to sleep in the back of the car, but had a restless night because I was aware the snake was there.

In my dream, the next day, the snake escaped from the car. I was too scared to go away from the car, in case the snake bit me. A friend tried to capture the snake, but he couldn't. Somehow, the snake got back into the car. This time I caught the snake and put it in a large hessian bag.

I rang Brad, my brother-in-law. I asked him what to do with the black snake. He said, "Take it to the theme park where there is a reptile enclosure. They'll take the snake." We went to the theme park together. I was wearing brand new blue shoes and a new lot of clothes, but I stepped into a deep puddle of water up to my knees, ruining the shoes.

A man from the snake enclosure came out to meet us. He looked inside the bag containing the snake. With awe he said, "That will be 9 big ones. $999,999 dollars." This is the amount he would pay me for the snake. I was shocked at such a high amount but when we looked in the bag, the black snake had multiplied and transformed into five awesome snakes, which were exotic, shiny and most spectacular to look at. The man shoved a large wad of cash into my hands and also gave me a golden orb, like those found on the top of some walking sticks.

The man said to me, "Go over to that hill in the distance and you will be shown what this orb is for." I went to the place the man indicated. A finely dressed gentleman came over and saw the golden orb in my hand. He got very excited and said, "This entitles you to two electric cars." He then showed me a deep blue Tesla model S, and a white Tesla model X. He also gave me a Tesla super-fast charger for our garage. (PS: My wife drives. I don't have a driving licence anymore. I handed it in during 2020 after seizures, myoclonic jerks, acute leg pain and spasms, all making it impossible for me to drive.)

When I got back home I gave a tithe to the Lord, that is, 10% of the money. I gave $100,000 dollars to

Platform 9, our church's arm for caring for disadvantaged and domestic violence victims. I also bought solar panels for our apartment block and a solar battery for all to share. Then the dream finished and I woke up full of joy.

My wife, Richelle spent considerable time and care interpreting the dream for me, praying for God's wisdom and using a Christian book about understanding dreams. I believe this is what the dream means.

- Stephen's life (represented by the Torana) has been written off.

- The black snake denotes a recurring curse or evil spirit which has been menacing him for a long time. The curse could be MS, or something else. (I believe the curse was pornography, as this is something I have battled with for much of my life). Each time it's caught, it escapes and returns. A friend tried to catch it but he failed, possibly meaning the prayers of others had not worked completely.

- Blue shoes show Steve is royalty. The shoes getting wrecked means Stephen has had to sacrifice a great deal in his life.

- Exotic snakes multiplying and an exorbitant payout indicate that God has transformed the curse into a blessing, far beyond what I could ever imagine or think. God has set me free form this curse and made my life beautiful again.

- Brad's advice was sought. Brad is a builder and manager. From his experience he often gives wise and Godly counsel to others.

- $999,999—The figure 9 denotes the end of the matter. This means the curse is finally and fully dealt with.

- Stephen's desire was to bless God, and others, as demonstrated by his giving money to God through Platform 9, along with the benefit of solar energy/battery and significant reduction in electricity costs given to our apartment block. God is providing him with the resources to bless others.

- The whole dream illustrates God's generosity. Stephen was given the cars he admires and desires, even though he can't drive—he was still happy! Stephen and Richelle are indeed blessed.

Chapter 9:

Lessons and Hope

I've learned to trust God again because He is faithful. He is still working with me. I have learned that God is good, though it's taken me a long time to really accept this. As I look back over my life, I can see his faithfulness, despite severe suffering and being unable to see it at the time.

I'm learning to accept the things I cannot change. When my body doesn't work the way, I want I now know I have a choice about how I respond. I can either get angry and frustrated, taking it out on those around me and voicing my complaints. Or I can accept that this is the way it is and not worry so much. I'm still practising this, but I can truly say life is calmer and better when I pull it off. My friend Irene said, "We are all a work in progress." This helps encourage me when life doesn't go the way I want. God hasn't finished with us yet and he is continually moulding us into the people he wants us to be.

I've learned to ask for what I need. We all need physical, mental, spiritual and emotional help at times because everyone has struggles and hard things to deal with in life. I am not alone in this. When I notice a new need for myself, I know who to contact to get support. Maybe a physiotherapist, a psychologist or an occupational therapist. I have a team who assist me to achieve my goals. These professionals have been invaluable in helping me progress and stay independent despite the challenges of MS.

I also ask for prayer when I need it. People all around the world pray for me all the time, which is very humbling. I'm very grateful for the many prayers for my life and health. My life is a prayer. I talk to God about what's on my mind every day and I believe he hears me and will answer. Nothing is too hard for God and I can be completely honest with him.

I've learned life is better when it's shared with people who love you. I feel so grateful to Richelle. She is a woman of great integrity who walks closely with Jesus Christ. She is very wise, quite intellectual and smart, and simply beautiful. Richelle is also my carer. We have been married for over 30 years and I am very grateful to God for her. My words cannot fully express what she means to me. I am also very grateful for my family and friends. Many have prayed for us and offered support in many practical ways.

I have been reminded that God is faithful and you can trust him to care for you. This doesn't mean everything will go well, but He will always be there. In parts of my life, God has been silent, however, I'm learning to hear God's voice again. I'm still struggling with this but my faith tells me that God was always with me, even though I felt strongly at the time that he was not.

As you can see, there have been a lot of things that have contributed to my life, some good, some not so good. I am still trying to live with MS, despite the many different reactions I have to God's ways. I don't have all the answers, but the bottom line is, I still trust God. I have his peace. I still trust that one day Jesus Christ will return and make things not just better, but completely new. I invite you to trust God with me to meet your needs.

I hold into this hope from Revelation 21:3-5, "Look, God's home is now among his people. He will live with them, and they will be his people. God himself will be with them. He will wipe every tear from their eyes, and there will be no more death or crying or pain. All these things are gone forever. And the One sitting on the throne said, "Look, I am making everything new!" (NLT)

His peace is about me and with me today. I am overwhelmed by God's grace and the many people he has brought into my life to help make daily living more bearable. God has led me through a deep valley and out the other side by His awesome hand. Praise His Name! I believe He can do the same for you and that whatever dark valley you may be in, take heart, it is only temporary. Much Grace.

.

www.ingramcontent.com/pod-product-compliance
Lightning Source LLC
Chambersburg PA
CBHW071744090426

42738CB00011B/2559